To Thomas—

Together We
Finish!

To learn more about Athletes Serving Athletes
visit www.athletesservingathletes.org

ISBN-10: 1541362411
ISBN-13: 978-1541362413

Printed in the United States
Amazon Create Space
*Created by Civin Media Relations*

# TOGETHER WE

Created by Todd Civin   Illustrated by Jason Boucher

# *Dedication*

This book is dedicated to Rick and Dick Hoyt, who served as the inspiration for ASA as well as the entire assisted running movement that has followed due to their efforts. I'd also like to dedicate this to all of our ASA Athletes, past, present and future.

~ David Slomkowski

*There comes a time in each man's life, as he gazes in the mirror,*

*Dreams to change the look that he reflects and see the world much clearer.*

David sat and watched a video,
Learned of a father and his son,

They changed the other's view of
life when the father helped him run.

Together We Fini

*"Dad, I don't feel disabled when the two of us compete,"*

*The son provided heart and soul, while he used his father's feet.*

*A tear raced down to David's chin as he rose up from his chair,*
*A fire grew inside of him; these words he hoped to hear.*

*Paced up the walls and 'round the room, wheels turning in his head,*

*"Why wasn't anyone doing this here?"  Finally drifted off to bed.*

He envisioned teams of Athletes with "WingMen" by their side,
Providing all with inspiration as each enjoyed their ride.

As the sun shined off the Chesapeake, it had never looked so pretty,
He may not change the entire world, but at least he could help his city.

*Walked through the doors of the William S. Baer to share what he had found,*
*As he left the school with their support; feet never touched the ground.*

*The birth of Athletes Serving Athletes as The Baer School loved his mission,*
*Help those with special abilities through athletic competition.*

*Though still without an Athlete,*
*never let it get him down,*
*Had faith that it would come to be*
*when James Banks rolled into town.*

*His mom gave him a pamphlet,*
*You don't want to do this, do ya?"*
*James hit the pavement on just two wheels,*
*arms waving; screaming*

### BOO-YAH!

*First race was a "Run to Remember" to honor heroes passed away,*

*To some may seem ironic that a new hero was born that day.*

*They ran the Baltimore Marathon; 26.2 long miles,*

*David ran, while King James screamed and produced a thousand smiles.*

With a bull horn or a cowbell; giving first bumps to the crowd,

"Never give up! Never Quit!" They heard him clear and loud.

No matter where they travel, James is recognized by face,

"We need to call the BFD. We just burned up this place!"

Whether in a chair, or in the boat
or biking at top speed,
Both the WingMan and the Athlete
fulfill the other's needs.

*It's the mission of the WingMan*
*and I'll try to keep this short,*
*Show the Athlete love,*
*significance, acceptance*
*while competing in the sport.*

BALTIMORE
COUNTY
BALTIMORE
CITY

HARFORD COUNTY
HOWARD COUNTY
Anne Arundel County

Together We Fini

*This is more than just a race for first in the sun or stormy weather,*

*It's the time between the two white lines to finish the race together.*

*Though James was the first  of ASA, so many deserve attention,*

*We'd love nothing more than*
*name them all,*
*but we've grown too large to mention.*

With ten areas 'round the region, each worthy of a look,
We hope you'll read about them all in a future ASA book.

We've space to meet a special few; or our story's not complete,
Shane Lauer and the Iron Girls, define the word compete.

*The face of our foundation; represents strength and grit and power,*
*Rolled into an incredible Athlete by the name of Shane C. Lauer.*

*He's the pride and joy of ASA; doors open as he arrives,*
*Our unofficial ambassador, brings inspiration to our lives.*

A man of very few spoken words,
 inspires others to achieve much more,
Courage, heart and dedication
when Shane rolls through the door.

Son of Ben and Carissa,
but like family to all others.
No water too deep, no mountain too steep,
when with ASA sisters and brothers.

Together We Fini

*Was the first to ride the ASA Bike; complete an Ironman distance race,*

*Whether with Dave or Chip or Ben or more; competition strained his face.*

Together We Fini

Became an accomplished painter;
shared his life view through his art,
Teaching us yet another lesson,
it's how you finish;
not where you start.

*"Go Big or Go Home"* was a belief he'd wear with pride,
To him each day was Ironman until the moment that he died.

Together We Fini

*Though Shane has since  departed, he'll be with us til the end,*

*Each time we roll out on a course, "Together We Finish for our friend."*

*Then there's Defu, Corey, Lily; the Iron Girls by name,*
*The spirit behind what ASA means and racing is their game.*

*Defu's smile is contagious; find a wall she'll roll right through it,*
*"The reason that I am on this earth is to show others they can do it."*

**Together We Finis**

*A mentor to the Iron Girls; you'll never see her lag,*
*A motivator to the WingMen, "We got this in the bag."*

*A reminder of what is possible; inspiring to me and you,*
*More than just an Iron Girl; she's Defu Fekadu.*

*And next in line is Corey; an Iron Girl from the start,*

*Her WingMan says, "Today I'm your legs; but you continue to be my heart."*

*A small tear travels down her face; as if it is her duty,*

*At roll call before every race; she witnesses the beauty.*

Today I'm your legs, but you continue to be my heart.

Not another one quite like her is a virtue most extol,

Shrugs her shoulders as she competes,

Says, "This is how we roll".

*See Corey has perspective as throughout the world we should. Despite the challenges she may face, her mantra's "It's all good."*

*The youngest of the Irongirls; wears a cute, pink sparkle skirt,*

*Is an Athlete named Lily; off playing in the dirt.*

*Shy and yet so confident; filled with determination,*

*As she rolls across the finish line with cheers of pure elation.*

*Lily's always sharing stories to get us through the miles,*
*Tells tales of crazy squirrels and fills us up with smiles.*

*She keeps the Irongirls going, right from the very start,*
*Don't judge the size of the athlete until witnessing her heart.*

More than just a racing group;
We're there to root each other on;
We're Athletes Serving Athletes;
It doesn't matter where
**Together We Finish!**

as happy as can be,
we're one big family.
our efforts will not diminish,
we start; as long as ...

# Real Life Scenes From Athletes Serving Athletes

*Ben, Chip and Dave enjoying some Shane time.*

*Looking good at the 2016 Raven's Run*

**The Historic Boston Marathon Finish Line**

*What we're all about at the ASA RunFest*

*Terrence Ridley at the Baltimore Triathlon*

*Shane Lauer with the First Place Medal
from the  Half Full Triathlon*

# Scenes from ASA RunFest 2016

*ASA Version of Where's Waldo?*

*Hans and Franz pumped up the crowd*

*Scooby Doo, Where Are You?*

*"Go Big or Go Home"*

**Bridge Run 2016**

# *Athletes Serving Athletes (ASA)*

**Mission:** *ASA empowers individuals living with disabilities to train and compete in mainstream running and triathlon events.*

**Why we do it:** *There are an estimated 666,000 people in the state of Maryland over the age of who have a form of disability.*

> *Approximately 120,000 people, or 2.4% of the state's population, experience difficulties with forming activities of daily living such as bathing, dressing, or moving around inside of homes.*

> *While sport has value in everyone's life, it is even more important in the life of a person with a bility. This is because of the rehabilitative influence sport can have not only on the phys body but also on rehabilitating people with a disability into society. Furthermore, sport teac independence.*

> *Our program serves as a catalyst to integrate individuals with disabilities into our community very profound and significant way. They get to feel the "thrill of competition" and enjoy a the benefits that come from participating in competitive sport.*

**How we do it:** *ASA pairs the athletes living with significant mobility challenges with able boc runners called "WingMen". Our WingMen are male and female, young and old, fast and slow. Wi Men push the athletes in custom racing joggers, rafts and bike pull behinds.*

**Where we do it:** *ASA is headquartered in Lutherville, Maryland and supports 10 areas ma throughout Maryland including: Baltimore County, Baltimore City, Carroll County, Harford Cou Howard County, Anne Arundel County, Eastern Shore (Salisbury), Frederick County, Southern Mc land, South Central P.A., with Montgomery County in the works.*

**When we do it:** *ASA's racing season starts in March, and continues until early Decemt In 2016 alone 185 ASA athletes (living with disabilities) have competed alongside 300+ WingMer over 90 main stream events, and have crossed the finish line 600+ times. All of our groups combi will host over 200 training sessions.*

addition to the 90+ events we competed in, ASA hosted the following in 2016:

Co-hosted the BaerAthlon with the administration of the William S. Baer School

3-day overnight bike trip on the Eastern Shore of Maryland

Supported Team Kevin at the 2016 Boston Marathon

Annual Trip to Ravens training camp in August

ASA 5k and Halloween Hustle in October

ASA Awards Program in January

ASA Bull Roast in March

**her Facts:**

Inspired by Rick and Dick Hoyt

Incorporated in 2008

Has an active 15-member Board of Directors that meets quarterly

2 full-time employees, 4 part-time employees, 4 interns per year

1000+ volunteers per year

To date, as a result of tremendous support, we have been able to offer our program free of charge to the individuals we serve!

# *TOGETHER WE FINISH!*

## A Complete List of our Incredible ASA Athletes

| Athlete's First Name | Athlete's Last Name | Community |
| --- | --- | --- |
| Andrew | Ablondi | Frederick County |
| Nadiya | Albrecht | Baltimore County |
| Jia Min John | Albrecht | Baltimore County |
| Thomas | Ampomah | Howard County |
| Morgan | Anchor | Howard County |
| Shaun | Badie | Baltimore County |
| Joshua | Badie | Baltimore County |
| Charlie | Bainbridge | Howard County |
| Natalie | Baker | Anne Arundel County |
| Molly | Baker | Anne Arundel County |
| Blake | Balciunas | Howard County |
| Benjamin | Balciunas | Howard County |
| James | Banks | Baltimore City |
| Zavion | Barnard | Eastern Shore |
| Joshua | Barrett Delclos | Baltimore County |
| Julia | Baur | Howard County |
| Elizabeth | Beall | Anne Arundel County |
| Robert | Beckman | Anne Arundel County |
| Lauren | Bell/Tinsley | Harford County |
| John | Bergey | Eastern Shore |
| Jessica | Bernstein | Eastern Shore |
| Scarlett | Birkmire | Frederick County |
| Rose | Birrane | Howard County |
| Emily | Black | Baltimore County |
| Ryan | Bozel | Baltimore County |
| Maggie | Breschi | Baltimore County |
| Ian | Brett | Eastern Shore |
| Amanda | Carroll | Baltimore County |
| Christian | Carter Proctor | Southern Maryland |
| Jackson | Clark | Baltimore County |
| Jeff | Coll | Other |
| Rebecca | Cooper | Anne Arundel Count |
| David | Crowley | Eastern Shore |
| Aiden | Cruse | Southern Maryland |
| Kenzi | Cullett | Baltimore County |
| Maddox | Dalyai | Frederick |
| Yusef | Darrehmane | Howard County |
| Caimile | Davis | Baltimore City |
| Nicholas | Davis | Eastern Shore |
| Benjamin | Davis | Eastern Shore |
| Byron | Deliyannis | Frederick |

| Athlete's First Name | Athlete's Last Name | Community |
|---|---|---|
| Nicolas | Deliyannis | Frederick |
| Jamison | Dickey | Anne Arundel County |
| Caryn | DiGiacomo | Baltimore County |
| Kelly | DiGiacomo | Baltimore County |
| Kevin | DiLegge | Baltimore City |
| Andrew | Donohue | Eastern Shore |
| Robb | Doub | Baltimore County |
| Christine | Downin | Harford County |
| Ryan | Drimal | Eastern Shore |
| Duane | Edwards, Jr | Baltimore County |
| Nathaniel | Epstein | Baltimore County |
| Damian | Evert | Eastern Shore |
| Connor | Farley | Harfor County |
| Guelila | Fekadu | Howard County |
| Alex | Fitzgerald | Howard County |
| Reginald | Fitzgerald | Baltimore City |
| Rebekah | Fleming | Eastern Shore |
| Jason | Ford Jr. | Baltimore City |
| Ian | Gallagher | Howard County |
| Norlan | Godshall | Baltimore County |
| George | Goodridge III | Eastern Shore |
| Ashley | Graffam | Frederick County |
| Dontae | Greene | PA |
| Max | Gretschel | Baltimore County |
| Landyn | Grove | PA |
| Noah | Hall | Eastern Shore |
| Sarah | Handy | Anne Arundel County |
| Ava | Hardy | Eastern Shore |
| Jerome Jonny | Harris | Frederick County |
| Savannah | Hinegardner | Baltimore City |
| Molly | Hodgetts | Baltimore County |
| Johnathan | Hoffaman | Baltimore County |
| Kimar | Holcey | Baltimore City |
| Clark Joe" | Hudak | Baltimore County |
| Gabrielle | Hurley-Johnson | Frederick County |
| Seamus | Huyette-Arrizza | Baltimore City |
| Regina | Jackson | Howard County |
| Kayleen | Kacsuta | Eastern Shore |
| Spencer | Keller | Howard County |
| Ryan | Kobylski | Howard County |
| Katherine | Kolm | Baltimore County |
| Chase | Kurtenbach | Howard County |
| Shane | Lauer | Baltimore County |

| Athlete's First Name | Athlete's Last Name | Community |
|---|---|---|
| Caleigh | Littin | Anne Arundel County |
| Gabriel | Little | Baltimore County |
| Ryker | Lyons | Eastern Shore |
| Nico | Maggio | Baltimore County |
| Ryan | Malone | Eastern Shore |
| Pazya | Margolis | Baltimore City |
| Victoria | Marsh | Newark/Wilmington/Middletown |
| Katie | Martin | Baltimore County |
| Danny | Marulanda | Lancaster PA |
| Jasir` | Massey | Eastern Shore |
| Raven | Matthews | Baltimore County |
| Kendall | May | Baltimore County |
| Shaunna | McBride | Baltimore City |
| Michael | McBride | Baltimore County |
| Sean | McDonough | Anne Arundel County |
| Joy | Meenan | Howard County |
| Graham | Mehl | Howard County |
| D'Andre | Midgette | Howard County |
| Helen | Miller | Lancaster or Philadelphia |
| Sophia | Mortenson | Baltimore County |
| Christopher | Mull | Eastern Shore |
| Leah | Mullen | Baltimore County |
| Tomás | Munoz | Baltimore County |
| Madeline | Mykins | Anne Arundel County |
| Nicholas | Nauman | Howard County |
| Ben | Newman | Howard County |
| Allison | Noonan | Howard County |
| Rachel | Nuckles | Carroll |
| Sarah | O'Keefe | Carrol County |
| Drew | Palmer | Howard County |
| Elijah | Palmer | Eastern Shore |
| Nathan | Pence | Baltimore County |
| David | Perry | Baltimore City |
| Nathan | Polkinghorn | Eastern Shore |
| Samari | Ponder | Frederick |
| Darren | Powell | Howard County |
| Larson | Pritchard | Frederick County |
| Saniyah | Pumphrey | Southern Maryland |
| Vincent | Rachels | Howard County |
| Nolan | Ramsey | Baltimore County |
| Kenna | Raynor | Frederick |
| Braxton | Reber | Baltimore County |
| Lily | Reckeweg | Eastern Shore |

| Athlete's First Name | Athlete's Last Name | Community |
|---|---|---|
| Ashley | Reeves | Central PA |
| Terrence | Ridley | Baltimore City |
| Kourtney | Rivers | Anne Arundel County |
| Alexa | Roberts | Frederick |
| Mason | Robinson | n/a |
| Lloyd | Rochez | Frederick |
| Meredith | Rodgers | Eastern Shore |
| Antoine | Rodgers | Baltimore City |
| Andrew | Ryan | Howard County |
| Nicholas | Sabo | Anne Arundel County |
| Katelyn | Sabo | Anne Arundel County |
| Brandon | Schaffer | Eastern Shore |
| Donna | Scharaga | Howard County |
| Zachary | Scherrer | Baltimore County |
| Bryce | Schnitzker | Baltimore County |
| Morgan | Schultz | Baltimore County |
| Cassidy | Scott | Howard County |
| Dominique | Sharpe | Howard County |
| Tommy | Shawhan | Howard County |
| Adam | Shuler | Baltimore County |
| Matthew | Shuler | Baltimore County |
| Jacob | Sittler | Baltimore County |
| Julian | Smith | Harford County |
| Kacie | Smith | Howard County |
| Nathan | Solano | Frederick |
| Jack | Sprague | Southern Maryland |
| Sam | Spring | Howard County |
| Joey | Sterling | Eastern Shore |
| Devin | Stine | Baltimore County |
| Leah | Street | Baltimore County |
| John | Suggs | Howard County |
| Megan | Tanner | Baltimore County |
| Sam | Taylor | Baltimore County |
| Marshall | Taylor | Baltimore County |
| Logan | Thomas | Eastern Shore |
| Jake | Thompson | Howard County |
| Aaron | Thornton | Howard County |
| Jesse | Trionfo | Baltimore County |
| Dan | Tucholski | Anne Arundel County |
| Arturo | Vallecillo-Rangel | Frederick County |
| Gabriel | Vazquez | Howard County |
| Frankie | Waldron | Baltimore County |
| Corey | Ward | Anne Arundel County |

## A Complete List of our Incredible ASA Athletes

| Athlete's First Name | Athlete's Last Name | Community |
| --- | --- | --- |
| Tyquon | Ward | Baltimore City |
| Tavon | Watson | Eastern Shore |
| Kyle | Weaver | Other |
| Ian | Weidenhammer | Central PA |
| Peter | Weston | Baltimore County |
| Dionze | White | Eastern Shore |
| Connor | Wolf | Rock Creek/ Frederick C |
| Luke | Wright | Howard County |
| Matthew | Wright | Baltimore County |
| Robert | Yoder | Baltimore City |
| Nate | Zahn | Howard County |
| Diego | Zetina | Eastern Shore |

## ASA Elite Sponsors

Baltimore Ravens
Melalueca Wellness Company
Gardiner Wolf Furniture

## ASA Sponsors

Alban CAT
Annapolis Striders
AquaCast Liner
Baltimore Ravens
Baltimore Police Department, City of Baltimore
Brown Advisory
CFG Community Bank
Charm City Run
Corrigan Sports Enterprise
Elite Race Management
Gardner Wolf Furniture
Glenwood Middle School
Grace Fellowship Church
Greenberg Gibbons
Grottos Pizza
IronMan Foundation
Koopers Tavern
Kelly Benefit Strategies
Law Offices of Howanski, Meadows & Erdman, LLC.
Mattingly & Associates
Melalueca Wellness Company
Mid Maryland Triathlon Club
Morgan Stanley
Mothers Grille
NTCI TeleAwareness
PANDORA Store, The Gallery at Harbor Place
RBC Wealth Management
Resource Enterprises, Inc.
Rip it Coaching

Rip It Events
Signal Hill
St. Patrick Celebrations, Inc.

The Marksmen Company
The William S. Baer School
Tributary Sourcing

## ASA Grantors

Bill and Louisa Wiener Fund
Civitan
Community Foundation, Eastern Shore
Ferris Family Foundation
Golfers Charitable Association
Haugh Family Charitable Foundation
Healey Family Foundation
Herbert Bearman Foundation
Hunts Church, Carrolls-Gill Endowment Fund

Marion I. and Henry J. Knott Foundation
Martin Richard Foundation
Oluv C. Joynor Foundation
PayPal Foundation
Perdue Farms, Inc.
Ronald McDonald Children's Charities
Transamerica Foundation
Wiessner Foundation for Children

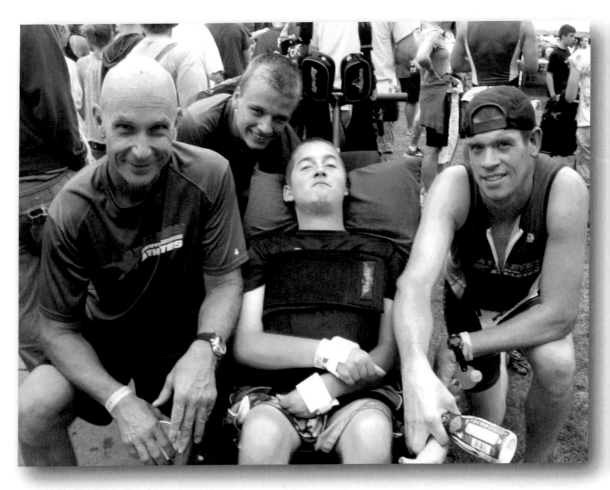

## Founding Board Members

Bill Gould — *Vice President Sales, Jim Boyd's Flooring America*

Geoff Miller — *Athletic Director, Goucher College*

Jeff Munson — *Senior Wealth Manager, RBC*

Cort Sandstrom — *President NTCI TeleAwareness/Sascomnet*

David Slomkowski — *Executive Director, Athletes Serving Athletes*

## Current Board Members

Mark Bomse — *Sr. Vice President Greenberg Gibbons Commercial*

Rob Gensler — *Retired, Portfolio Manager T. Rowe Price*

Dr. Laura Harlan — *Emergency Room Doctor Northwest Hospital*

Kristine Howanski — *Managing Partner Howanski, Meadows & Erdman, LLC*

Chris Kennedy — *Teacher Loyola Blakefield*

Kevin McNulty — *Vice President Chair, Development Committee Resource Enterprises, Inc.*

Geoff Miller — *Secretary Athletic Director Goucher College*

Mark Monahan — *VP Sales and Marketing Aquacast*

Stephen Moritz — *President VP Sales EMC*

Bill Wiedel — *Treasurer Chief Financial Officer CFG Community Bank*

Steven Book — *Associate Attorney Kramon & Graham, P.A.*

Justin Huovinen — *Tax Manager SC&H Group, LLC*

Melinda Peters — *Senior Director RK&K*

Melissa Goldmeier — *Assistant County Solicitor Howard County Office of Law*

## ASA Staff

| | |
|---|---|
| David Slomkowski | Executive Director |
| Sarah Slomkowski | Director of Operations |
| Lisa Cooper | WingManager |
| Aimee Rogers | Athlete Manager |
| Eleanor Maranto | Office Administrator |
| Julia Kardian | Special Event Coordinator |

## Volunteer Area Coordinators

| | |
|---|---|
| Christina Beaverson | Harrisburg- South Central PA |
| Kerry Blackmer | Frederick County |
| Stephanie Blades | Howard County |
| Emily Cole | Baltimore City |
| Lisa Cooper | Baltimore County |
| Jill Fears | Eastern Shore-Salisbury |
| Christine Johnson | Baltimore City |
| I. Monet Ouwinga, MD | Southern Maryland |
| Jen Roussillon | Anne Arundel County |
| Kate Sumrow | Harford County |

*Front Row Left to Right: Stephanie Blades, Aimee Rogers, Christina Beaverson, Kerry Blackmer*
*Back Row Left to Right: Kate Sumrow, Lisa Cooper, Sarah Slomkowski, Emily Cole, Jill Fears,*
*Christine Johnson  Middle Row standing on phone books: Jen Roussillon*

ut the author: **Todd Civin** is a husband, father of five and grandfather of three to
. He is a graduate of Syracuse University Newhouse School of Public Communica-
s. Civin is the founder and CEO of Civin Media Relations and is the Social Media Di-
or for the Kyle Pease Foundation. He is the co-author of **One Letter at a Time** by Rick
t and Todd Civin, **Destined to Run** by Wes Harding and Todd Civin, **Just My Game** by
n Grilli and Todd Civin and **Love in the Trenches of Everyday Life** by Jose Vazquez
Todd Civin. He is also the author and creator of children's books **Where There's a
eel There's a Way** and **A Knight in Shining Armor and A Bike to Call Their Own** He
verjoyed to add **Together We Finish!** to his resume.


ut the artist: **Jason Boucher** is an artist and mason. He has been in construction go-
on 16 years but has been an artist most of his life. He never took a lesson and is pretty
h self-taught. He's married to his beautiful wife Erika and they have a beautiful
ghter named Kayla and two handsome sons, Beau and Blake. It's his goal to be a full
illustrator and finally throw the work boots away! Together Todd and Jason have col-
orated on seven books with plans for several more in the coming year.

www.athletesservingathletes.org

Made in the USA
San Bernardino, CA
05 January 2017